10 HABITS OF HIGHLY EFFECTIVE TRADERS

Transform Your Trading Journey
with Proven Principles

GODFX

Copyright © 2024 GODFX

All rights reserved

The characters and events portrayed in this book are fictitious. Any similarity to real persons, living or dead, is coincidental and not intended by the author.

No part of this book may be reproduced, or stored in a retrieval system, or transmitted in any form or by any means, electronic, mechanical, photocopying, recording, or otherwise, without express written permission of the publisher.

ISBN-13: 9798342050852
ISBN-10: 1477123456

Cover design by: Art Painter
Library of Congress Control Number: 2018675309
Printed in the United States of America

To all the determined traders who dare to break boundaries and chase the dream of financial freedom. May this book guide you through the challenges, ignite your passion, and empower you to build a future of wealth and purpose—not just for yourselves, but for the generations to come.

To the mentors and educators who generously share their wisdom, shaping the future of trading with their insights and support. Your commitment creates a legacy of success, ensuring the growth of the trading community and its lasting influence.

And to my family and friends, whose encouragement and belief have been my greatest strength. Your faith in me has fueled my ambition, and your love has given me the courage to pursue my dreams. This journey is ours together, and I am forever grateful.

"Success in trading isn't found in the pursuit of perfection, but in mastering the habits that lead to consistent execution. A trader's edge lies not in predicting the market, but in disciplining the mind."

— *GODFX*

THIS BOOK IS DEDICATED TO THE COUNTLESS TRADERS WHO HAVE SHARED THEIR INSIGHTS, SUCCESSES, AND FAILURES. WITHOUT THE EXPERIENCES OF THE TRADING COMMUNITY AND THE WISDOM OF THOSE WHO CAME BEFORE US, MASTERING THE MARKETS WOULD BE AN EVEN GREATER CHALLENGE. EVERY LESSON LEARNED, EVERY HABIT ADOPTED, IS BUILT ON THE SHOULDERS OF TRADERS PAST AND PRESENT.

CONTENTS

Title Page

Copyright

Dedication

Epigraph

Foreword

Introduction

Preface

Prologue

Untitled

HABIT 1: Master the Basics, Constantly	1
HABIT 2: Develop a Routine	6
HABIT 3: Never Stop Learning	13
HABIT 4: Keep Emotions in Check	19
HABIT 5: Stay Patient	25
HABIT 6: Stay Humble	34
HABIT 7: Manage Risk Like a Professional	39
HABIT 8: Risk What You Can Afford to Lose	45
HABIT 9: Review and Reflect on Every Trade	50
HABIT 10: Adapt and Innovate	55
Epilogue	61
Afterword	63

Acknowledgement	65
About The Author	67
Praise For Author	69
Books In This Series	71
Books By This Author	73
Books By This Author	75
Untitled	77

FOREWORD

In the realm of trading, where the line between success and failure can be razor-thin, the importance of effective habits cannot be overstated. I have had the privilege of witnessing numerous traders embark on their journeys, each bringing their unique perspectives and strategies to the markets. Yet, through my years of experience, one truth remains constant: the most successful traders share a common thread—a set of habits that distinguishes them from their peers.

When I first met GODFX, it was clear that he possessed not only an exceptional understanding of the markets but also a genuine passion for sharing knowledge. His journey is a testament to the idea that success is not solely determined by intelligence or analytical skills; rather, it is the disciplined and consistent application of certain habits that truly leads to mastery in trading.

In "10 Habits of Highly Effective Traders," GODFX distills his hard-earned wisdom into practical, actionable insights. Each habit outlined in this book is rooted in real-world experiences—both triumphs and setbacks—that will resonate with traders at any stage of their journey. From fostering discipline to cultivating a growth mindset, these habits are essential tools that will empower you to navigate the complexities of trading with confidence.

As you read through the pages of this book, I encourage you to reflect on your own trading practices and consider how these habits can be integrated into your daily routine. Success in trading is not a destination but a continuous journey of learning and growth. By embracing the principles laid out in this book, you will be well-equipped to turn challenges into opportunities and develop the mindset needed to thrive in the ever-changing landscape of the financial markets.

GODFX's insights will inspire you, challenge you, and ultimately transform the way you approach trading. This book is more than just a guide; it is a roadmap to becoming a highly effective trader. I invite you to embark on this journey with an open mind and a commitment to personal growth. The habits you cultivate today will shape your success tomorrow.

— GODFX

INTRODUCTION

Trading can be one of the most rewarding pursuits, offering financial freedom and the ability to take control of your life. But for many, it becomes a source of frustration and disappointment. Too often, traders find themselves caught in a cycle of highs and lows—excited by their wins, only to be crushed by the inevitable losses that follow. The truth is, the markets are unforgiving, and success doesn't come from luck, instinct, or even technical analysis alone. It comes from adopting the right habits.

The habits of highly effective traders are what separate those who thrive in the markets from those who barely survive. These traders aren't immune to mistakes or losses, but they've learned how to manage risk, remain disciplined, and develop a long-term mindset that consistently works in their favor.

This book is about those habits—the daily practices and mindsets that transform ordinary traders into successful ones. It's about the shift from reacting to the market's every move to controlling your responses with a calm, focused approach. These are habits that anyone can learn, but they require dedication, patience, and a willingness to change your trading behavior.

In **"10 Habits of Highly Effective Traders,"** we'll explore each of these habits in detail, from mastering risk management and controlling emotions to developing a disciplined trading routine. You'll learn how to create a solid trading plan and stick to it, how to avoid the emotional traps that lead to costly mistakes, and how to approach the markets with the mindset of a seasoned pro.

Whether you're just starting out or looking to improve your

current performance, this book will provide you with actionable strategies that can help you build a sustainable and successful trading career. By the end, you'll not only understand what the most effective traders do—you'll have the tools to join their ranks.

Success in trading doesn't happen by accident. It's the result of consistently making the right decisions, and that starts with building the right habits.

Let's get started.

— GODFX

PREFACE

Trading is often seen as a journey toward financial independence, but for many, it can feel more like a battleground of emotions, uncertainty, and losses. When I first started, I made every mistake imaginable—overtrading, chasing the market, letting my emotions control my decisions. I learned the hard way that trading isn't just about mastering strategies or analyzing charts—it's about mastering yourself.

This book, **"10 Habits of Highly Effective Traders,"** is the result of years of trial and error, growth, and reflection. Through my own experiences and observing countless successful traders, I've come to realize that consistent habits, not talent or luck, are the foundation of long-term success in the markets.

The habits outlined in this book are designed to help traders of all levels build the discipline, mindset, and strategies necessary to navigate the markets confidently. Whether you're a beginner or an experienced trader looking to sharpen your edge, these habits will guide you toward more consistent performance, better decision-making, and, ultimately, greater success.

I've written this book because I know firsthand how frustrating and overwhelming trading can be without the right tools. My goal is simple: to help you avoid the mistakes that so many traders fall victim to and to give you the habits you need to become a highly effective trader.

Trading is not just about mastering the markets—it's about mastering yourself. And with the right habits, you can do just that.

Welcome to the journey.

— GODFX

PROLOGUE

In the ever-evolving landscape of financial markets, trading is often portrayed as a high-stakes game—a thrilling rollercoaster ride of wins and losses. Yet, beneath the surface excitement lies a world governed by principles, habits, and unwavering discipline. As a trader who has navigated this turbulent journey, I have learned firsthand that success is not merely a matter of luck or intuition but rather the result of cultivating specific habits that set effective traders apart from the rest.

Throughout my years in the markets, I have experienced both the exhilarating highs of triumph and the sobering lows of failure. Each experience, whether positive or negative, has shaped my understanding of what it truly means to be an effective trader. I have witnessed how certain habits can propel individuals to greatness, while others can lead to ruin. This book distills those lessons into ten essential habits that I believe every trader must adopt to thrive in the financial world.

In these pages, I will share not only the strategies that have worked for me but also the mistakes I've made along the way. My goal is to illuminate the path for aspiring traders, helping them avoid the pitfalls I encountered and guiding them toward success. Whether you are a novice taking your first steps or an experienced trader seeking to refine your approach, these habits will provide you with a solid foundation for mastering the art of trading.

As you embark on this journey with me, I invite you to reflect on your own trading practices. Consider how adopting these habits can transform your mindset, enhance your decision-making, and ultimately lead you to the success you seek. Let us dive into the world of trading, where the right habits can turn ambition into achievement and dreams into reality.

— GODFX

UNTITLED

HABIT 1: MASTER THE BASICS, CONSTANTLY

"Success in trading isn't about knowing everything—it's about mastering the essential things that matter the most." – GODFX

In the fast-paced world of trading, it's easy to get caught up in the pursuit of the next big strategy or the latest trading technology. But after years of navigating the markets, I've learned one crucial truth: mastery comes from consistently refining the basics.

When I first started, like many traders, I was obsessed with finding the "secret" to beating the market. I'd spend hours researching complex indicators, new strategies, and trading algorithms. I wanted to unlock the shortcut to success. But the more I traded, the more I realized that even the most sophisticated strategies wouldn't work without a solid foundation. That foundation is built on mastering the basics.

Why the Basics Matter

The core principles of trading—risk management, technical analysis, understanding market psychology—are timeless. Whether you've been trading for six months or six years, these fundamentals will never change. What sets successful traders apart from the rest is not the number of indicators on their chart, but their ability to stick to the basic principles that consistently work.

You wouldn't expect to become a grandmaster in chess without understanding how each piece moves or mastering the opening moves of the game. Trading is no different. You must constantly revisit and refine your understanding of the fundamentals. I call this the "Foundational Cycle." Every successful trader goes through this cycle repeatedly to stay sharp.

Let me break it down:

1. Risk Management:

This is the backbone of trading. You can have the best strategy in the world, but if you don't manage your risk properly, one bad trade can wipe you out. For me, risk management means never risking more than 1-2% of my total account balance on a single trade. This may sound conservative, but it's what has kept me in the game long-term.

Early in my career, I ignored this advice and paid the price. I remember a time when I was overly confident in a trade, risking close to 10% of my account. The trade didn't go as planned, and that loss hit hard, both financially and emotionally. After that, I committed to never violating my risk management rules again.

2. Technical Analysis:

Technical analysis is the study of price charts and patterns. It's one of the most powerful tools you can use to predict market movements. But here's the thing: you don't need to know every pattern, indicator, or technique out there. Focus on mastering a few key indicators—such as moving averages, support and resistance levels, and candlestick patterns—and use them consistently.

For me, simplicity works best. I rely heavily on moving averages to spot trends and look for key support and resistance levels to time my entries and exits. When you master the basics of technical analysis, it becomes easier to read the markets without being overwhelmed by too much information.

3. Market Psychology:
If there's one area of trading that is often overlooked, it's understanding market psychology—both your own and the market's. The market is driven by fear, greed, and emotion. Being aware of this dynamic can help you avoid emotional decision-making and take advantage of opportunities when others are panicking or euphoric.
I can't count how many times I've seen traders give up because they were either too emotional or didn't recognize what was driving the market at the time. If you can control your emotions and understand how sentiment affects market movements, you'll have a significant edge over the competition.

Revisiting the Basics
Now that we've established why the basics are important, let's talk about how to *constantly* revisit them.
No matter how experienced you become, never assume you've "graduated" from the fundamentals. I make it a point to refresh my knowledge of the basics regularly—especially during market downtime. Here's how I do it:

1. Monthly Review Sessions
Every month, I dedicate a few hours to review the core concepts that drive my trading strategy. I go over my risk management plan, recheck my understanding of the key technical indicators I use, and study market psychology. This practice keeps my knowledge sharp and reminds me that these basics are the foundation of my success.

2. Journaling
Journaling isn't just for tracking trades. I use it as a way to review whether I've adhered to my basic principles in each trade. Did I manage my risk correctly? Did I follow the technical signals without letting emotions dictate my decisions? By reflecting on each trade, I can see where I might have deviated from the

fundamentals and correct those mistakes going forward.

3. Backtesting Simple Strategies
Backtesting is when you apply your trading strategy to historical data to see how it would have performed in the past. I make it a point to go back and test simple, basic strategies on historical charts. This practice not only strengthens my understanding of the fundamentals, but also keeps me confident in their effectiveness.

How Mastering the Basics Made Me the No.1 Trader
You might be wondering—how did mastering the basics help me become the world's No.1 trader? It wasn't about finding the most complex strategy or being glued to the screen all day. It was about consistency, discipline, and mastering the essential concepts that most traders overlook.

Early in my career, I tried to bypass the basics and get to the "advanced stuff." I wanted fast success. But after losing significant amounts of money on risky trades, I realized that the traders who were consistently successful all had one thing in common—they respected and mastered the fundamentals.

By mastering risk management, I could trade with confidence, knowing that even if a trade didn't work out, my losses would be contained. By refining my technical analysis, I could make quick, informed decisions about when to enter or exit trades. And by understanding market psychology, I was able to stay calm and avoid making impulsive, emotional decisions.

Actionable Steps for You
So how can you start mastering the basics? Here are some practical steps to implement right away:

1. Create a Risk Management Plan:
Define your maximum risk per trade (e.g., 1-2% of your account). Stick to this no matter what.
Set a daily or weekly loss limit. If you hit it, stop trading for that

period.

2. Master 1-2 Key Technical Indicators:
Pick 1-2 indicators (e.g., moving averages, support and resistance, or candlesticks) and learn them inside and out.
Practice identifying these patterns in historical charts to build confidence in your ability to spot them in real-time.

3. Study Market Psychology:
Pay attention to market sentiment. Is the market fearful? Overconfident? Use this knowledge to avoid emotional trades.
Work on self-awareness. Track how emotions influence your decisions and commit to staying disciplined.

4. Revisit the Basics Regularly:
Set a recurring schedule for reviewing risk management, technical analysis, and market psychology. Make it part of your routine.
Mastering the basics doesn't just make you a good trader; it makes you a consistent trader. It's the difference between hoping for profits and expecting them. Keep revisiting, refining, and reinforcing these core principles, and you'll set yourself up for long-term success in the markets.

HABIT 2: DEVELOP A ROUTINE

"Success in trading is not just about the trades you make—it's about the routine that shapes the mindset and discipline behind those trades." – GODFX

In the trading world, consistency is everything. The markets are unpredictable, often chaotic, and constantly changing. What separates great traders from the rest isn't just their knowledge of the market or their strategies—it's their routine. A routine is the backbone that supports your trading discipline, focus, and mental clarity.

Over the years, I've developed a strict daily routine that keeps me grounded. It's not just about what I do when I'm trading, but also about how I prepare before and how I reflect afterward. This routine ensures that I'm always at my best—mentally, physically, and emotionally—so I can make clear, informed decisions in a market that is anything but stable.

The Power of Routine in Trading
When I first started trading, I didn't have a routine. I would open my laptop, stare at the charts, and wait for the market to show me an opportunity. I was reactive, not proactive. This approach led to impulsive decisions, missed opportunities, and emotional trades. I quickly realized that if I wanted to succeed long-term, I needed

to approach trading with structure and discipline—just like a professional athlete prepares for a game.

Developing a routine transformed my trading. I stopped reacting to the market and started preparing for it. My routine became my anchor, helping me stay consistent, even on the most volatile days. It gave me a sense of control, even when the markets were unpredictable.

My Daily Trading Routine

Let me walk you through my routine. It's the framework I follow every day to ensure I'm mentally sharp, well-prepared, and emotionally balanced before I enter any trade.

1. Pre-Market Preparation: The Calm Before the Storm

Every successful trader starts their day well before the market opens. I like to think of this as the "calm before the storm." The time before the market opens is sacred—it's when I prepare my mind, review the news, and make a game plan for the day ahead. Here's how my pre-market routine works:

Wake Up Early:

My day starts at least two hours before the market opens. I use this time to wake up slowly, have a nutritious breakfast, and mentally prepare for the day ahead. Trading is mentally exhausting, and starting the day rushed and stressed can cloud your judgment.

News & Global Markets:

After breakfast, I review the major financial news outlets to see what's happening globally. I check for any economic reports, geopolitical events, or market-moving news that could affect the day's trading session. This gives me a broader context of what to expect from the market.

I also glance at other major markets like Europe and Asia to get a sense of how they've performed. Often, these markets provide clues for how the U.S. markets may react when they open.

Market Sentiment:
Sentiment is key. I check sentiment indicators and market mood from pre-market trading activity, futures contracts, and any early movements in major indices. Is the market leaning toward fear or greed? Is it in risk-on or risk-off mode? Knowing the market's overall sentiment helps me frame my strategy.

Review Open Positions:
Before placing any new trades, I always review my current open positions. I assess their performance, check stop-loss levels, and determine if adjustments are needed. This ensures that I'm aware of any risks or opportunities with my ongoing trades.

Set Daily Goals:
I set realistic, manageable goals for the day. Sometimes the goal is as simple as being patient and waiting for the perfect setup. Other times, I may set profit targets or risk management objectives. My goals aren't always about making money—they're about trading well and maintaining discipline.

2. Market Opening: Execution with Precision
When the market opens, there's often a burst of volatility. Novice traders get caught up in the chaos, but seasoned traders know how to navigate this initial wave calmly. My routine keeps me centered and focused on my plan rather than reacting emotionally to every market move.

First 30 Minutes: Observation Mode
When the market first opens, I rarely make trades. The opening bell brings a lot of volatility as traders react to overnight news or pre-market activity. I spend the first 30 minutes in observation mode, watching how the market responds, and identifying trends or opportunities. Jumping in too early often leads to bad decisions.

Execute Pre-Planned Trades:

If I have pre-planned trades based on my pre-market analysis, I execute them calmly and methodically. My trades are based on a combination of technical indicators, price action, and the market sentiment I analyzed before the opening bell.

Stick to the Plan:
One of the most important elements of my routine is sticking to the plan I created before the market opened. I never deviate unless new information or a significant market event occurs. This helps prevent emotional decision-making and keeps me disciplined.

3. Midday Routine: Reflection and Adjustment
The middle of the trading day often sees a lull in market activity, known as the "midday doldrums." This is the perfect time to reflect on the trades you've made so far and adjust your plan for the rest of the day.

Review Morning Trades:
Around midday, I take time to review the trades I've made. Did they align with my plan? Was my entry and exit strategy sound? Reflection is a key part of my routine because it helps me learn from each trade, regardless of whether it was a win or a loss.

Check News for Updates:
I do another check of the financial news to see if anything has changed since the morning. Sometimes a new piece of information can completely alter the market's direction, so staying informed is crucial.

Reassess Market Conditions:
The market can shift quickly. I reassess the technicals, sentiment, and overall direction of the market to see if I need to adjust my trading plan for the afternoon. This part of the routine ensures that I'm staying nimble and adaptive to the evolving market.

4. Post-Market Routine: Reflection and Analysis

Once the market closes, my work isn't done. The post-market routine is one of the most important parts of my day because it's where I reflect on the decisions I made, analyze the outcomes, and prepare for the next day.

Journaling:
After the market closes, I always spend at least 30 minutes journaling my trades. I record why I entered a trade, how I felt during the trade, what the outcome was, and whether I stuck to my plan. This process helps me recognize patterns in my behavior—both good and bad—that I can use to improve my future performance.

Review of Open Positions:
If I have open positions that I'm holding overnight, I review them thoroughly. I check for any risks or news that could affect their performance and ensure my stop-losses and profit targets are in place.

Daily Self-Assessment:
I ask myself: How did I perform today? Did I follow my routine? Did I let emotions affect my trades? Self-assessment is a powerful tool for personal growth, and I make it a point to reflect on my performance, not just the market's.

Plan for Tomorrow:
Lastly, I spend time planning for the next trading day. I analyze potential setups for the next day based on what happened in the market, review my ongoing trades, and adjust my trading strategy if necessary. This preparation allows me to enter the next day's trading session with confidence.

Why Routine is Critical for Consistency
Routine brings consistency, and consistency is the foundation of long-term success in trading. When you follow a routine, you're not just reacting to the market—you're approaching it with a clear

mind, a well-defined plan, and the discipline to execute that plan without letting emotions take control.

Without a routine, you're at the mercy of the market's unpredictability. You'll find yourself jumping into trades impulsively, chasing profits out of fear or greed, and making decisions that don't align with your overall strategy. Trust me—I've been there, and it doesn't work.

How Routine Has Transformed My Trading Career

Let me give you a real example of how my routine saved me from disaster.

A few years ago, during a highly volatile market event, I had pre-planned my trades based on my routine. I'd done the research, prepared mentally, and created my strategy for the day. When the market opened, there was chaos—price swings were extreme, and traders around the world were panicking.

Because of my routine, I was able to stay calm and follow my plan. I didn't let the noise affect me. I waited patiently for the right setup and executed my trades with precision. While many traders were losing money due to emotional decisions, I came out with a profit because I trusted my routine.

Actionable Steps for You

Now that you understand the importance of developing a routine, here are some steps to help you build one for yourself:

1. Create a Pre-Market Routine:

Wake up early, check the news, review global markets, and set daily goals before the market opens. Make this part of your morning ritual.

2. Have a Trading Plan Ready:

Plan your trades before the market opens, including your entry and exit points, and the amount of risk you're willing to take on. Write it down.

3. Observe the Market Before Trading:
Spend the first 30 minutes of the trading day observing market behaviour before jumping into trades. Let the initial volatility settle.

4. Midday Reflection:
Use the midday lull to review your trades and check the news for any updates. Adjust your plan if necessary.

5. Post-Market Review:
After the market closes, journal your trades and reflect on your performance. Use this time to learn from your mistakes and successes.

6. Prepare for Tomorrow:
Plan your trades for the next day and analyze any ongoing positions to ensure you're ready for the next session.

By developing a structured routine, you're not just preparing yourself for the trading day—you're setting the foundation for long-term success. Routine breeds discipline, and discipline is what separates winning traders from those who get lost in the chaos of the markets.

HABIT 3: NEVER STOP LEARNING

"The market is a never-ending classroom. To stay ahead, you must remain a student for life." – GODFX

If there is one truth in trading that I've learned, it's that the markets are constantly evolving. What works today might not work tomorrow. Strategies that were effective last year may become obsolete as new market dynamics emerge. This is why learning in trading is not optional—it's a necessity.

Every day the market teaches you something new. It might be about a particular asset, a pattern, or even about yourself. Those who thrive in trading are not necessarily the most talented or intelligent; they are the ones who are committed to learning and adapting. This chapter will dive into why continuous learning is critical, how it has shaped my career, and actionable ways you can adopt the mindset of a lifelong learner.

Why Learning is the Lifeblood of Trading Success

When I started trading, I had a lot of confidence. I thought I knew enough to beat the markets, but I quickly learned how little I really knew. The market humbled me again and again, teaching me hard lessons that I could have avoided had I committed to learning and improving.

You see, trading is an ongoing process. The markets are influenced by numerous factors—global events, technological advances, changes in market sentiment, and new financial instruments. No matter how skilled you are, if you're not constantly upgrading your knowledge, you'll eventually fall behind.

Here's the thing: The markets don't care about your ego. They don't care if you were successful last month or last year. If you don't evolve with them, you'll get left behind. The traders who survive—and thrive—are those who commit to learning for the long haul.

Learning Through Experience: My Greatest Teacher
While there are countless books, courses, and seminars on trading, experience is by far the best teacher. I've learned more from my mistakes than I ever did from reading a book or watching a webinar. The key is to treat every trade, every success, and every failure as an opportunity to learn.

Let me give you an example.

A few years ago, I was trading during a time of heightened market volatility. I'd studied market patterns, felt confident in my technical analysis skills, and made a series of trades that ended up losing me a significant amount of capital. Naturally, I was frustrated, but instead of wallowing in defeat, I used that experience to learn. I went back, reviewed the trades, analyzed what went wrong, and adjusted my strategy. That single losing streak taught me more about risk management and market dynamics than any book could.

The takeaway here is that experience—whether positive or negative—is one of the most powerful learning tools in a trader's arsenal. But to truly benefit from it, you must be willing to reflect on your experiences and draw lessons from them.

The Markets Are Evolving: Are You?
In the past decade, trading has undergone a radical transformation. The rise of algorithmic trading, the growing influence of social media, and the introduction of cryptocurrencies have created new opportunities and challenges

for traders. Staying on top of these changes requires a commitment to learning.

The financial markets of today are more complex than ever before. New technologies like AI and machine learning are impacting trading strategies, while geopolitical events create unpredictable movements across markets. In this rapidly changing environment, you can't afford to be static. To stay competitive, you must continually expand your knowledge and evolve your strategies.

Here are a few areas where continuous learning is crucial:

Technology and Trading Tools:
Modern trading is heavily reliant on technology. From algorithmic trading platforms to advanced charting tools, keeping up with the latest tech is essential. I'm constantly learning about new trading tools, automation strategies, and how to leverage them in my trades. Technology is a game-changer if you know how to use it effectively.

Global Economic Trends:
The world economy is interconnected, and global trends can have a significant impact on market behavior. Staying informed about macroeconomic trends, central bank policies, and global financial news helps me anticipate market movements. I make it a habit to read up on global economics daily to keep my strategies relevant.

New Markets and Instruments:
Cryptocurrency, decentralized finance (DeFi), and non-fungible tokens (NFTs) are just a few examples of new financial markets and instruments that have emerged. Even if you're not actively trading these assets, understanding them helps you stay ahead of the curve. Knowledge of these new opportunities can open doors to new strategies and profitable trades.

Market Sentiment and Behavioural Finance:
Markets are driven by human behaviour—fear, greed, uncertainty,

and euphoria all play a role in price movements. Studying market sentiment and understanding the psychology behind it helps me anticipate trends and avoid common traps. Behavioural finance is an area I continuously study because it allows me to understand the emotional drivers behind market movements.

Learning from Others: Mentors, Peers, and Resources
One of the biggest accelerators of my growth as a trader was learning from others. I sought out mentors, connected with experienced traders, and immersed myself in trading communities where I could exchange ideas and insights. I learned from their mistakes, borrowed strategies, and adapted their wisdom to my own trading style.

Mentorship is a powerful tool in trading. A good mentor can help you avoid pitfalls, refine your strategy, and challenge your thinking. If you can, find someone who has been in the market longer than you and has seen its various cycles. Their experience will be invaluable.

In addition to mentors, I regularly engage with my peers—traders who are at different stages of their journey. Trading can be an isolating profession, but having a network of like-minded individuals helps you stay motivated, learn new strategies, and keep a pulse on market sentiment.

Books, podcasts, and online courses are also valuable resources. I've read countless trading books and continue to do so. However, I approach them with a critical mind. Not every strategy or piece of advice will work for me, but each one provides insight and a new perspective that I can evaluate and test.

Turning Learning into Action: Application is Key
Knowledge alone won't make you a successful trader—application is key. I've seen traders who spend hours learning about the market but never implement what they've learned. Information without action is wasted.

In my journey, I've adopted a "learn, test, apply" approach. Whenever I learn a new concept or strategy, I test it out in a small, controlled environment. I'll paper trade the strategy or use a demo account to see how it performs in real market conditions. If it works, I'll slowly integrate it into my broader trading plan.

For example, when I first learned about algorithmic trading, I didn't just read about it—I spent weeks developing simple algorithms and testing them in real-time. By applying what I learned, I was able to incorporate algorithmic strategies into my trading routine, which has significantly improved my consistency and execution.

Overcoming the Fear of the Unknown
One of the biggest barriers to continuous learning is the fear of the unknown. New markets, new technologies, and new strategies can feel intimidating. I've met traders who stick to what they know because they're afraid to step out of their comfort zone.

However, the greatest breakthroughs in my trading career came from venturing into unfamiliar territory. I embraced cryptocurrencies when they were still new, I explored algorithmic trading before it was mainstream, and I adopted new risk management techniques when the market conditions demanded it.

The lesson here is simple: Don't be afraid to learn something new, even if it feels overwhelming at first. The markets reward those who are willing to adapt and innovate.

Building a Learning Plan: How to Stay Ahead
To stay sharp and evolve as a trader, I've built a learning plan that keeps me focused on growth. Here's how you can do the same:

1. Set Learning Goals:
Every quarter, I set specific learning goals. It could be mastering a new trading tool, studying a market I've never traded, or deepening my understanding of a specific strategy. Having clear goals keeps me focused and accountable.

2. Schedule Time for Learning:

In the same way you schedule time for trading, you should schedule time for learning. I dedicate at least 30 minutes a day to reading, watching webinars, or studying charts. Consistency is key.

3. Test New Strategies:
Whenever I learn something new, I test it before incorporating it into my trading plan. This could be through paper trading or using a demo account. The goal is to see how the strategy performs in real market conditions without risking capital.

4. Engage with the Trading Community:
Whether through online forums, social media groups, or in-person meetups, engaging with other traders keeps you informed and inspired. I regularly participate in trading discussions to exchange ideas and stay updated on new trends.

5. Reflect and Adjust:
Continuous learning also means being reflective. Every week, I take time to reflect on what I've learned, how it has impacted my trading, and whether I need to adjust my approach. Reflection helps me turn knowledge into action.

The Infinite Game of Trading
In many ways, trading is an infinite game. There is no final destination—no point where you can say, "I've learned everything." The markets are constantly shifting, and as a trader, you must remain a student of the game for life.
By adopting a mindset of continuous learning, you position yourself to not only survive but thrive in the ever-changing landscape of trading. Embrace the fact that you'll never know everything and that there is always more to learn. This humility, combined with a relentless pursuit of knowledge, is what will set you apart as a trader.

HABIT 4: KEEP EMOTIONS IN CHECK

"In trading, your worst enemy isn't the market—it's your emotions. Master them, and you'll master the game." – GODFX

One of the hardest lessons I've learned in my trading career is that the market doesn't care about your feelings. It doesn't care if you're excited about a potential breakout or devastated by a sudden loss. The market is cold, indifferent, and unpredictable. And if you let your emotions, take control, you'll make mistakes—sometimes devastating ones.

As traders, we're human. We experience fear, greed, frustration, and euphoria. These emotions can cloud our judgment and lead to poor decision-making. Over the years, I've discovered that mastering your emotions is one of the most important skills a trader can develop. It's not just about making the right trades—it's about making the right trades consistently, without being swayed by emotional highs and lows.

In this chapter, I'm going to share why emotional control is critical in trading, how it has impacted my performance, and specific techniques that have helped me manage emotions when the market gets chaotic.

Why Emotions Are Your Biggest Threat

In the trading world, emotions like fear and greed are notorious for causing traders to deviate from their strategies. It's natural to feel elated after a big win or fearful after a loss, but these emotions can wreak havoc on your trading if you allow them to influence your decisions.

Greed: The Silent Killer of Discipline

Greed often manifests when a trader is on a winning streak. After a series of successful trades, it's easy to get overconfident and take excessive risks. I've seen it happen time and time again—even with seasoned traders. You start to believe that you can do no wrong, and this belief can lead to poor decisions.

I've been guilty of this too. I remember a period in my career where I made several successful trades back-to-back. My confidence soared, and I started ignoring my own risk management rules, thinking I could handle bigger positions. It worked…until it didn't. One large loss wiped out nearly all my previous gains, reminding me that greed had clouded my judgment.

The lesson here is simple: Never let greed drive your decisions. It's tempting to push your luck when you're winning, but in the long run, undisciplined behavior will lead to losses.

Fear: The Enemy of Opportunity

On the opposite end of the spectrum is fear. After a loss, it's natural to feel hesitant about entering another trade. Fear can paralyze you and prevent you from taking action, even when the right setup presents itself. This fear of losing again can stop you from seizing profitable opportunities.

There was a time early in my career when a few bad trades in a row left me questioning my abilities. I became overly cautious, hesitant to pull the trigger on trades that met all my criteria. By the time I convinced myself to act, the market had already moved, and the opportunity was gone.

Fear is a natural response to losses, but it must be managed if you want to remain a consistent trader. Trading from a place of fear will only cause you to miss opportunities and undermine your confidence.

The Consequences of Emotional Trading
When emotions dictate your trades, you enter a dangerous cycle:

1. Overconfidence leads to larger-than-necessary risks.

2. Fear leads to missed opportunities and stunted growth.

3. Frustration after losses leads to revenge trading—trying to "win back" losses, often resulting in more losses.

4. Euphoria from a big win can lead to reckless, uncalculated trades.

In my early trading days, I experienced all of these. I made impulsive decisions out of greed and fear, leading to significant losses. It took me years to realize that emotional trading is not sustainable. The key is learning to trade with a clear, objective mind—free from emotional interference.

The Role of Psychology in Trading
Most new traders underestimate the importance of trading psychology. They focus heavily on learning technical analysis, fundamental analysis, or mastering strategies—thinking that's all they need. But here's the truth: Your mindset will make or break you in the markets.

In fact, I'd argue that trading is 80% psychology and 20% strategy. Even with the best strategy in the world, if you can't manage your emotions, you will struggle. The best traders aren't necessarily the ones with the most complex strategies—they're the ones who can keep their cool in high-pressure situations and stick to their plan.

Trading as a Mental Game
Trading requires mental resilience. You must accept that losing trades are part of the game. No one has a 100%-win rate, and the best traders know this. They embrace losses as opportunities to learn and improve, instead of letting them trigger emotional

responses.

I've spent years developing the mental toughness needed to deal with the emotional ups and downs of trading. When you can master your emotions, you can make objective decisions based on data and analysis—not impulse or panic.

How I Learned to Keep My Emotions in Check

It wasn't easy for me to learn how to control my emotions in trading. It took time, discipline, and practice. Here are some of the techniques that helped me manage my emotions, and that I believe can help any trader maintain control:

1. Trade with a Plan, Not on Impulse

This is one of the most important steps to keeping emotions in check. Before entering a trade, I always have a clear plan that includes my entry point, exit point, and stop-loss level. I know my risk-to-reward ratio and the reasons behind each trade.

By following a structured trading plan, I remove emotional decision-making from the equation. I don't chase trades just because the market looks exciting, and I don't panic-sell when the market moves against me. Instead, I trust my plan and let it guide my actions.

2. Set Realistic Expectations

I've learned that unrealistic expectations are a breeding ground for emotional trading. When you expect every trade to be a winner, you're setting yourself up for disappointment—and that disappointment can lead to rash decisions.

Trading is not about hitting home runs every time. It's about consistently making good decisions that generate profit over time. By setting realistic expectations, I stay grounded and avoid the emotional rollercoaster that comes with expecting perfection.

3. Use Risk Management to Reduce Emotional Stress

One of the biggest reasons traders let emotions take over is because they're risking too much. If you're putting a large portion of your capital into a single trade, you're going to feel emotional pressure, whether you realize it or not.

That's why I always stick to strict risk management rules. I never risk more than a small percentage of my total capital on any single trade. This way, if a trade goes against me, it's not emotionally devastating. I can stay calm and objective because I know that no single trade will make or break me.

4. Take Breaks to Reset

If I feel myself getting emotional during a trading session—whether it's from frustration after a loss or excitement after a win—I take a break. Stepping away from the screen gives me the space I need to reset my mindset and regain control of my emotions.

This practice of taking breaks has saved me from making impulsive decisions countless times. The market will always be there when I come back, and it's better to miss a trade than to make a bad one driven by emotion.

5. Practice Mindfulness and Meditation

Mindfulness and meditation have become essential tools in my emotional management toolkit. These practices help me stay present, focused, and aware of my emotional state throughout the trading day. By being mindful of my emotions, I can recognize when I'm about to decide based on impulse and take steps to prevent it.

Every morning, before I start my trading day, I spend 10 minutes meditating. This helps me clear my mind and approach the market with a calm, focused attitude. I also practice mindfulness during the day, taking deep breaths and refocusing when I feel stress or excitement creeping in.

6. Keep a Trading Journal

A trading journal has been one of the most valuable tools in my emotional growth as a trader. I document every trade I make—not just the numbers, but my thoughts, emotions, and reasoning behind each trade.

By reviewing my journal regularly, I can see patterns in my behavior. I can identify moments where emotions influenced my decisions and learn from them. This helps me improve my emotional control over time and become more disciplined in my approach.

Learning to Accept Losses
One of the biggest emotional challenges in trading is accepting losses. No one likes to lose money, but in trading, losses are inevitable. The key is to accept them, learn from them, and move on without letting them affect your future decisions.
Early in my career, I struggled with accepting losses. I would hold onto losing trades for too long, hoping the market would turn in my favor. I couldn't accept that I was wrong, and this emotional attachment to my trades led to even bigger losses.
Now, I've learned to embrace losses as part of the process. I treat every loss as a learning experience and don't dwell on it. I've realized that it's not about being right or wrong—it's about managing risk and staying disciplined.

Turning Emotional Control Into a Competitive Advantage
Here's the truth: Most traders struggle with emotional control. They let fear, greed, and frustration drive their decisions, and it costs them. But if you can master your emotions, you'll have a significant edge over the majority of traders.
Emotional control allows you to stay calm in volatile markets, stick to your plan, and avoid the costly mistakes that come from impulsive decisions. It's a skill that can take you from being a mediocre trader to a highly effective one.
In my experience, emotional control is the foundation of long-term success in trading. It's not something you develop overnight—it takes time and practice. But once you master it, you'll find that the market becomes less intimidating, and your trading decisions become more consistent and profitable.

HABIT 5: STAY PATIENT

"Patience is not just a virtue in trading—it's a necessity. It separates the disciplined from the impulsive, and the profitable from the reckless." – GODFX

In trading, we're constantly looking for the right moment—the perfect setup that aligns with our strategy, risk management, and market conditions. But here's the hard truth: the market doesn't always move on your schedule. Opportunities don't come when you want them to. That's where patience comes in.

Many traders, especially those who are new to the game, fall into the trap of over-trading. They believe that more trades mean more profits, but that mindset is often a fast track to failure. True success in trading comes not from trading frequently, but from trading wisely—and that requires patience.

In this chapter, I want to discuss the critical role that patience plays in my trading strategy, how it has saved me from making costly mistakes, and the steps you can take to develop patience as a core component of your trading discipline.

Why Patience is Critical in Trading

It took me a long time to realize that patience is one of the most important habits a trader can develop. When you're patient, you give yourself the space to make clear, well-thought-out decisions. When you're impatient, you rush into trades without proper analysis, chasing quick profits that rarely come.

Here's the reality: the market rewards those who wait for high-probability setups. It doesn't matter if you're day trading, swing trading, or investing for the long term—timing is everything. And patience is what allows you to wait for that right moment.

Avoiding the Trap of Over-Trading

When I first started trading, I had this belief that if I wasn't in a trade, I was wasting time. Every day, I would look for setups—even if they didn't meet my criteria—just to feel like I was making progress. This led to a lot of impulsive trades, and more often than not, they resulted in losses.

The problem with over-trading is that you're constantly reacting to short-term movements rather than sticking to your strategy. Instead of waiting for the perfect setup, you start convincing yourself that *any* setup is good enough. This mindset is dangerous and usually ends with traders blowing their accounts.

I remember a specific phase in my career when I over-traded during a highly volatile market. I ignored my plan, thinking that I could profit from the fast-moving price swings. The result? Several losses in a row. It was a hard lesson that taught me the value of waiting for the right trade rather than chasing every little opportunity.

The Market Will Always Be There

One of the most calming realizations for me was that the market isn't going anywhere. There will always be another opportunity. Just because you missed one setup doesn't mean your trading career is over. In fact, rushing into a trade because you're afraid of missing out (FOMO) is a recipe for disaster.

By developing patience, I learned to accept that it's okay to sit on the sidelines and wait for the right moment. Trading is a game of probability, and patience allows you to wait for setups that offer the highest chances of success.

The Power of Waiting for High-Probability Setups

One of the habits that has contributed most to my success is the ability to wait for high-probability setups. What do I mean by that? A high-probability setup is a trade that meets all of your pre-defined criteria: technical analysis, market conditions, risk-reward ratio, and personal strategy.

But here's the catch: these setups don't come around every day. Sometimes, you'll go days or even weeks without seeing a perfect setup. During those periods, it's tempting to jump into suboptimal trades just to "do something." That's where patience comes in.

When you have the discipline to wait for high-probability setups, you trade less often but with far greater success. Your trades become more calculated, and your overall performance improves because you're only entering the market when the odds are truly in your favor.

Patience in Action: One of My Key Trades
There was a time in my career when I was watching a specific financial instrument that had shown signs of an impending breakout. The technical analysis was clear, but the timing wasn't right yet. My strategy indicated that I should wait for a particular support level to be tested before entering.

For days, I watched the price move up and down, testing my patience. At several points, I was tempted to jump in early, thinking I could predict the breakout before it happened. But I held back and waited for the right moment.

Finally, the price hit the support level I'd been watching, and the indicators lined up perfectly. I entered the trade with confidence, knowing I had waited for the highest-probability setup. Within a few days, the price broke out, and I made a substantial profit.

This experience reinforced for me that waiting for the right setup —no matter how long it takes—pays off. Trading isn't about taking action constantly; it's about taking the right action at the right time.

How Impatience Can Lead to Costly Mistakes
The opposite of patience is impatience, and I've seen firsthand how dangerous it can be in trading. Impatient traders are more

likely to enter trades that don't align with their strategy, over-leverage their positions, and hold onto losing trades for too long.

When you're impatient, you start to chase the market instead of letting the market come to you. You jump into trades without proper analysis, hoping to catch a quick win. But this mindset often leads to poor decisions and, ultimately, losses.

Impatience also manifests in the form of revenge trading—trying to quickly recover from a loss by entering another trade right away. I've been there. After a significant loss early in my career, I immediately entered another trade, thinking I could win back what I'd lost. That second trade was driven by emotion, not logic, and it only led to more losses.

Practical Steps to Develop Patience in Trading

Patience is a skill that can be learned, but it requires conscious effort. Here are some practical steps I've used to develop patience in my trading:

1. Define Your Criteria for Entering and Exiting Trades

One of the best ways to cultivate patience is by having clearly defined criteria for entering and exiting trades. When you have specific rules in place, you're less likely to act impulsively.

For example, my criteria for entering a trade include a certain combination of technical indicators, market conditions, and risk-reward ratios. If a trade doesn't meet all of these criteria, I simply don't take it. By following this rule, I remove the temptation to jump into trades that don't align with my strategy.

2. Focus on the Long Game

Trading is not a get-rich-quick scheme. It's a long-term endeavour that requires consistency, discipline, and patience. When you focus on the long game, it becomes easier to wait for high-probability setups and avoid impulsive decisions.

I remind myself constantly that my goal is not to make money on every trade but to build consistent, sustainable profits over time. This mindset shift helps me stay patient, even when the market is slow.

3. Practice Meditation and Mindfulness
Meditation and mindfulness have played a huge role in my ability to stay patient in trading. These practices help me stay calm and centered, even during periods of market volatility. By training my mind to stay present, I'm less likely to make decisions driven by impatience or fear.

Every morning before I start trading, I spend 10-15 minutes meditating. This helps me approach the market with a clear, focused mind. I also use mindfulness techniques throughout the day, especially when I feel the urge to act impulsively.

4. Journal Your Trades
Keeping a trading journal is a powerful way to develop patience. When you document your trades, you can review them later and identify patterns in your behavior.

For example, after reviewing my journal, I realized that most of my losses came from trades I entered too early because I was impatient. By recognizing this pattern, I was able to work on waiting for the right setups and avoiding premature entries.

5. Set Alerts and Walk Away
One of the most effective strategies I've developed for staying patient is setting alerts and walking away from the screen. Instead of sitting there staring at the market, waiting for a setup, I set alerts on key price levels and indicators. This way, I'm notified when the market reaches my predetermined conditions, and I can act accordingly.

This strategy prevents me from overanalysing the market and making emotional decisions out of boredom or impatience.

The Role of Patience in Risk Management
Patience also plays a critical role in risk management. When you're patient, you're more likely to stick to your risk management rules, wait for the right risk-reward ratio, and avoid

taking unnecessary risks. Impatient traders, on the other hand, often over-leverage their positions in the hopes of making quick profits, which can lead to devastating losses.

By practicing patience, you can manage your risk more effectively and protect your capital over the long term.

The Impact of Patience on Trading Psychology

In trading, psychological factors can significantly influence performance. A trader's mindset, emotions, and overall psychological state can often dictate their success or failure. Patience is a cornerstone of effective trading psychology. It allows you to remain composed during times of uncertainty and navigate the inevitable ups and downs of the market.

Building a Resilient Mindset

Developing a resilient mindset requires practice and awareness. Here are some strategies to help you cultivate patience and resilience in your trading:

1. Acknowledge Your Feelings: It's normal to feel anxious, excited, or even fearful when trading. Instead of trying to suppress these emotions, acknowledge them. Recognizing your feelings allows you to address them constructively without letting them dictate your decisions.

2. Visualize Your Success: Take time to visualize yourself successfully waiting for and executing high-probability trades. By reinforcing this positive imagery in your mind, you can build confidence in your ability to remain patient.

3. Practice Self-Compassion: Trading is filled with challenges, and you will inevitably face losses. Treat yourself with compassion during these times, acknowledging that every trader experiences setbacks. Understand that patience is a skill that takes time to develop.

Case Study: The Power of Waiting for Market Reversals
One of my most memorable trading experiences revolved around a significant market reversal. I had been watching a major currency pair that was in a prolonged downtrend. Many traders around me were eager to short the currency, believing the trend would continue indefinitely.

Instead of jumping in, I chose to wait for signs of a potential reversal. I studied the price action closely, analysing support levels and looking for confirmation through various technical indicators.

After several days of watching and waiting, the market finally showed signs of strength with a bullish candlestick pattern that indicated a reversal. I entered the trade with confidence, knowing that I had waited for a high-probability setup rather than reacting impulsively.

As the market rallied, I was able to ride the trend up, securing a profitable position. This experience reinforced the lesson that patience can lead to significant rewards when trading.

Balancing Patience with Proactivity
While patience is essential, it's equally important to strike a balance between waiting for the right setups and being proactive in your trading education and analysis. Here's how to achieve this balance:

1. Be Active in Your Learning: Use periods of waiting to enhance your skills and knowledge. Study market trends, analyze historical data, and engage with trading communities to expand your understanding of market behavior. This proactive approach ensures that when the right opportunity arises, you're prepared to act.

2. Set Clear Goals and Milestones: Establish short-term and long-term trading goals that align with your overall strategy. Setting milestones gives you something to work towards during periods of waiting, keeping your motivation high without sacrificing patience.

3. Stay Engaged Without Overtrading: Monitor the market, but resist the urge to enter trades without clear justification. Use technical analysis tools and charts to stay informed about potential setups. This engagement can provide valuable insights while still allowing you to remain patient.

Creating a Patience Plan

To solidify the role of patience in your trading, consider developing a "Patience Plan." This plan can serve as a guide for how you approach trading with patience at the forefront. Here's a simple outline to help you create your own:

1. Define Your Trading Strategy: Clearly outline your trading strategy, including your criteria for entry and exit, risk management rules, and preferred timeframes. This clarity allows you to remain focused and patient.

2. Set Trade Frequency Limits: Decide on a maximum number of trades you're willing to take in a week or month. This limitation encourages you to be more selective with your trades and reinforces patience.

3. Establish a Review Schedule: Set specific times for reviewing your trades, strategies, and market conditions. Use these reviews to assess your adherence to patience, analyse your performance, and make necessary adjustments.

4. Incorporate Breaks: Allow yourself scheduled breaks from trading. This could be a day or even a week where you step back from the markets. This time away can help you recharge, reflect, and return with a renewed sense of patience.

Conclusion: Embracing Patience as a Trader

Patience is more than just waiting; it's about being intentional in your trading decisions. It's recognizing that the market is a marathon, not a sprint. By embracing patience, you allow yourself the space to make thoughtful decisions and capitalize on high-probability setups.

Incorporating patience into your trading routine will not only enhance your performance but also make your trading experience more enjoyable. Remember, successful trading is not solely about winning; it's about making consistent, informed decisions that align with your strategy.

As you move forward in your trading journey, I encourage you to embrace patience fully. The market will reward you for it, and you'll find yourself growing not just as a trader but as a disciplined investor.

HABIT 6: STAY HUMBLE

"Success in the market is never guaranteed—stay humble, because the moment you believe you've conquered it, the market will remind you who's in charge."-GODFX

In the world of trading, success can often lead to a false sense of invincibility. The thrill of profitable trades and the accolades from peers can inflate one's ego, creating a mindset that is detrimental to long-term success. Staying humble is not just a personal virtue; it's a fundamental principle that can safeguard your trading journey and ensure sustainable growth.

The Nature of Humility in Trading
Humility in trading encompasses a few essential aspects:

1. Acknowledging Limitations: Every trader has strengths and weaknesses. Recognizing your limitations is crucial in preventing overconfidence and blind spots. No one can predict the market with absolute certainty, and acknowledging this reality can keep you grounded.

2. Learning from Mistakes: Every trader will encounter losses and setbacks. Humility allows you to accept these experiences as opportunities for growth rather than viewing them as failures. A humble trader learns from mistakes, refining their strategies and decision-making processes.

3. Respecting the Market: The financial markets are complex and often unpredictable. Humility involves understanding that the market can change rapidly and that what worked yesterday may not work today. This respect for the market keeps you vigilant and adaptable.

The Psychological Impact of Humility
Humility plays a significant role in shaping a trader's psychological landscape:

1. Reducing Emotional Bias: Humble traders are less likely to be influenced by their emotions, such as greed or fear. When you maintain a humble attitude, you're more likely to make rational decisions based on data and analysis rather than reacting impulsively to market movements.

2. Encouraging Continuous Learning: A humble mindset fosters a desire to learn. Humility drives traders to seek knowledge, engage with mentors, and pursue education, which enhances their skills and keeps them updated on market trends and strategies.

3. Promoting Resilience: The trading journey is fraught with challenges and setbacks. A humble trader is better equipped to bounce back from losses, as they understand that setbacks are part of the learning process. This resilience is vital for long-term success.

Strategies for Cultivating Humility
Cultivating humility is a continuous journey. Here are several actionable strategies to foster a humble mindset in your trading practice:

1. Adopt a Growth Mindset: Embrace the belief that your abilities can be developed through dedication and hard work. Understand that mastery in trading is a journey that requires continuous improvement and adaptation. Celebrate your progress, but never let it cloud your judgment.

2. Keep a Trading Journal: Document your trades, including your thought process, outcomes, and emotions. Reviewing your journal regularly can provide insights into your decision-making patterns and areas for improvement, reinforcing humility by reminding you of your mistakes and successes.

3. Seek Feedback and Mentorship: Engage with other traders, whether through forums, social media, or trading groups. Be open to constructive criticism and different perspectives. Mentorship can be invaluable, as seasoned traders can provide insights and lessons from their own experiences.

4. Practice Gratitude: Regularly take time to reflect on the opportunities you have as a trader. Whether it's the access to information, the ability to trade from anywhere, or the community of fellow traders, practicing gratitude can help you stay grounded and humble.

5. Set Realistic Expectations: Understand that trading is not a guaranteed path to wealth. Set realistic goals for your trading journey and be prepared for the ups and downs. Acknowledging the inherent risks of trading can keep you humble and focused on the long-term process.

Real-Life Example: A Lesson in Humility
Let me share a story that illustrates the importance of humility in trading:
Early in my trading career, I experienced a string of successful trades that filled me with confidence. I was hitting my targets consistently, and the adrenaline rush of winning became addictive. I started to take larger positions, believing that my winning streak would continue indefinitely.
However, my overconfidence led me to overlook crucial market

signals. I ignored the economic indicators that suggested a potential downturn, convinced that my skills would shield me from any losses. I took a significant position based on a hunch rather than solid analysis.

I quickly learned that the market does not bend to the will of individual traders. The price reversed sharply, leading to a substantial loss that wiped out a significant portion of my profits. This experience was humbling and forced me to confront my overconfidence.

From that point on, I made a conscious effort to stay humble. I began to seek feedback from experienced traders, reviewed my trading plan, and re-evaluated my strategies. I recognized that every market cycle is different, and humility is crucial in navigating them.

Balancing Confidence with Humility

While humility is vital, it's also essential to balance it with confidence. Here's how to achieve that equilibrium:

1. Trust Your Analysis: Confidence in your trading plan and analysis is crucial. Humility does not mean doubting yourself; it means recognizing that you can always improve. Trust your skills while remaining open to learning and adapting.

2. Embrace Challenges: View challenges as opportunities to grow rather than threats to your competence. A humble yet confident trader approaches obstacles with curiosity and determination, seeing them as steppingstones to greater success.

3. Celebrate Your Wins Modestly: When you achieve success, celebrate it without boasting. Share your wins with others in a way that encourages and inspires rather than inflates your ego. This approach fosters a supportive trading community and reinforces humility.

Conclusion: The Power of Humility in Trading

In conclusion, staying humble is an indispensable trait for traders seeking long-term success. Humility allows you to recognize your limitations, learn from mistakes, and adapt to the ever-changing market landscape. By cultivating humility, you create a strong foundation for your trading journey, enabling you to make rational decisions and navigate challenges with resilience.

As you continue to grow and develop as a trader, remember that humility will serve as your compass, guiding you through both the highs and lows of your trading career. Embrace this virtue, and you'll find yourself not just surviving in the markets but thriving over the long haul.

HABIT 7: MANAGE RISK LIKE A PROFESSIONAL

"To trade like a pro, manage risk first—profits follow those who protect their capital."-GODFX

In the world of trading, the difference between success and failure often boils down to how well a trader manages risk. Risk management is not just a protective measure; it is the cornerstone of a sustainable trading career. Professional traders understand that every trade carries inherent risks, and the ability to manage these risks effectively is what sets them apart from amateurs.

Understanding Risk in Trading
Before diving into risk management strategies, it's essential to grasp what risk means in the context of trading:

1. Market Risk: The possibility of losing money due to adverse price movements in the market. Market risk can arise from various factors, including economic events, geopolitical issues, and changes in market sentiment.

2. Liquidity Risk: This refers to the risk of not being able to execute trades at desired prices due to insufficient market activity. Illiquid markets can lead to larger price swings, amplifying potential losses.

3. Credit Risk: Involves the risk of loss arising from a counterparty's inability to meet its obligations. This is particularly relevant in trading derivatives and bonds.

4. Operational Risk: The risk of loss from inadequate or failed internal processes, systems, or external events. This includes technical failures, human errors, and fraud.

The Importance of Risk Management
Effective risk management is essential for several reasons:

1. Preserving Capital: The primary goal of any trader is to preserve their trading capital. Without effective risk management, even the best trading strategies can lead to significant losses that can wipe out an account.

2. Enhancing Decision-Making: A clear risk management strategy helps traders make informed decisions based on objective criteria rather than emotions. This structured approach encourages discipline and consistency.

3. Long-Term Sustainability: Trading is a marathon, not a sprint. A sound risk management plan ensures that traders can withstand the inevitable ups and downs of the market, allowing them to continue trading over the long term.

Key Principles of Risk Management
To manage risk like a professional, consider the following key principles:

1. Determine Your Risk Tolerance: Every trader has a different risk tolerance based on their financial situation, trading experience, and psychological comfort. Before entering any trade, assess how much you are willing to risk and set clear boundaries.

2. Use Stop-Loss Orders: Stop-loss orders are essential tools for managing risk. By setting a predetermined exit point for a losing trade, you can protect your capital and prevent emotional decision-making. Ensure your stop-loss orders are strategically placed based on technical analysis rather than arbitrary levels.

3. Position Sizing: Calculate the appropriate position size for each trade based on your risk tolerance and account size. A common rule is to risk no more than 1-2% of your trading capital on a single trade. This approach ensures that even a series of losses won't significantly impact your overall account.

4. Diversification: Spread your risk across multiple assets or markets. Diversification helps reduce exposure to any single investment and mitigates the impact of adverse price movements in one area.

5. Regularly Review and Adjust: Continuously assess your risk management strategies and adjust them based on market conditions, your trading performance, and any changes in your risk tolerance. Regularly reviewing your approach keeps you adaptable and responsive to evolving circumstances.

Psychological Aspects of Risk Management
Risk management is as much about psychology as it is about strategy. Understanding the psychological factors at play can help traders adhere to their risk management plans:

1. Fear and Greed: Fear of losing money can lead traders to exit positions too early, while greed can cause them to take unnecessary risks. A solid risk management plan can help mitigate these emotional influences, keeping traders focused on their strategies.

2. Overconfidence: After a series of successful trades, it's easy to become overconfident. This mindset can lead to increased risk-taking and ignoring risk management principles. Regularly reviewing your trades and sticking to your risk management plan can help keep overconfidence in check.

3. Cognitive Dissonance: This psychological phenomenon occurs when a trader's beliefs conflict with their actions. For instance, a trader may believe in their strategy but fail to stick to their risk management plan. Recognizing and addressing cognitive dissonance can help reinforce discipline.

Practical Strategies for Effective Risk Management
Here are practical strategies to enhance your risk management practices:

1. Develop a Risk Management Plan: Create a detailed plan that outlines your risk tolerance, position sizing rules, stop-loss strategies, and diversification approach. Having a written plan provides clarity and helps you stay disciplined during trading.

2. Utilize Risk-Reward Ratios: Assess the potential reward of a trade relative to the risk taken. A common guideline is to aim for a risk-reward ratio of at least 1:2, meaning that for every dollar risked, you should aim to make two dollars. This approach helps ensure that your winning trades outweigh your losing trades over time.

3. Monitor Economic Indicators: Stay informed about key economic indicators and events that may impact the market. Understanding these factors can help you make informed decisions about your trades and manage risk accordingly.

4. Practice Risk Management in Simulated Trading: Before applying new risk management strategies in real trading, practice them in a simulated trading environment. This practice can help you become comfortable with your approach without risking real capital.

5. Conduct Post-Trade Analysis: After each trade, analyze the outcome to determine if your risk management strategies were effective. Assess whether your stop-loss was appropriately placed and if your position size was aligned with your risk tolerance. This analysis can help you refine your approach and improve future performance.

Case Study: A Lesson in Risk Management
Let me share an example from my own trading experience that highlights the importance of effective risk management:
Early in my career, I came across a promising financial instrument that had just announced a breakthrough product. Excited by the news and the potential for profit, I invested a significant portion of my capital without fully assessing the risks. I believed that the price would continue to rise, and I neglected to set a stop-loss order.
Within days, the price began to decline due to broader market concerns, and I watched helplessly as my capital diminished. I realized that I had failed to adhere to my risk management principles, which ultimately cost me dearly. This experience was a turning point, leading me to prioritize risk management in every trading decision.
From that day forward, I developed a comprehensive risk management plan, set stop-loss orders for all my trades, and implemented strict position sizing rules. By learning from my mistakes and focusing on risk management, I was able to rebuild my trading account and achieve long-term success.

Conclusion: The Path to Professional Risk Management
In conclusion, managing risk like a professional is essential for sustaining a successful trading career. Effective risk management practices protect your capital, enhance decision-making, and contribute to long-term sustainability in the market.
As you navigate the complexities of trading, remember that every

decision carry risk. By prioritizing risk management and adhering to established principles, you empower yourself to make informed choices and minimize potential losses.

Ultimately, successful trading is not just about making profits; it's about managing risk effectively and developing a disciplined approach to every trade. Embrace risk management as a fundamental pillar of your trading strategy, and you'll find yourself on the path to achieving your financial goals with confidence.

HABIT 8: RISK WHAT YOU CAN AFFORD TO LOSE

"True trading success lies in understanding that every investment carries risk; protect your capital by only risking what you can afford to lose, and let the markets reward your wisdom."– GODFX

In trading, the concept of risk is a fundamental principle that distinguishes successful traders from those who struggle to stay afloat. One of the most essential rules every trader must internalize is to only risk what they can afford to lose. This principle is not merely a caution; it is a vital strategy that can safeguard your trading career and ensure your financial well-being.

Understanding the Principle
The essence of risking only what you can afford to lose is grounded in the reality of the trading environment:

1. Market Unpredictability: Financial markets are inherently unpredictable, influenced by numerous factors, including economic indicators, geopolitical events, and market sentiment. Understanding this unpredictability is crucial to mitigating the risks involved.

2. Your Financial Situation: Each trader has a unique financial situation, which includes personal expenses, savings, and obligations. Risking funds that are essential for daily living or financial stability can lead to catastrophic consequences.

3. Preserving Capital: The primary goal of trading is not to make a fortune overnight but to preserve and grow your capital over time. By only risking what you can afford to lose, you create a safety net that allows you to trade with confidence, even in turbulent market conditions.

The Psychological Impact of Risking What You Can Afford to Lose

The mindset of only risking what you can afford to lose has profound psychological implications:

1. Reduced Anxiety: When you know that you are only risking disposable income, it alleviates the stress associated with trading. This clarity allows you to make decisions based on logic and analysis rather than fear and anxiety.

2. Enhanced Focus: Knowing that your financial exposure is limited allows you to concentrate on your trading strategy without the distractions of worrying about significant losses. You can make decisions based on market conditions and your trading plan.

3. Long-Term Perspective: A mindset centered around responsible risk management fosters a long-term perspective. Instead of seeking immediate gains, you become focused on sustainable growth, allowing for a more patient and disciplined approach to trading.

Strategies for Risking What You Can Afford to Lose

Here are practical strategies to help you adopt this essential habit:

1. Create a Trading Budget: Establish a specific trading budget that outlines how much money you can allocate to trading without impacting your financial stability. This budget should be separate from your living expenses and savings, ensuring that you are not risking essential funds.

2. Set Clear Risk Limits: Determine your risk tolerance on a per-trade basis. A common guideline is to risk only 1-2% of your total trading capital on any single trade. This rule ensures that even if you face a series of losses, your account balance remains intact.

3. Utilize a Separate Trading Account: Consider maintaining a separate trading account specifically for your trading activities. This separation can help you delineate between your trading funds and personal finances, making it easier to manage risk responsibly.

4. Avoid Using Margin: Trading on margin can amplify both gains and losses. If you are new to trading, it's advisable to avoid using margin until you are more experienced and confident in your trading strategies. Relying on your capital rather than borrowed funds minimizes the risk of significant losses.

5. Practice Risk-Reward Ratios: Before entering any trade, calculate the risk-reward ratio. Aim for a minimum ratio of 1:2 or better, ensuring that potential gains outweigh potential losses. This approach can help you identify high-probability trades while limiting financial exposure.

The Dangers of Overextending Yourself
Understanding the dangers of risking more than you can afford is crucial for maintaining a healthy trading approach:

1. Emotional Turmoil: Risking funds that you cannot afford to lose can lead to emotional turmoil, fear of loss, and irrational decision-making. When your financial well-being is at stake, it can be challenging to remain objective and disciplined.

2. Chasing Losses: When faced with significant losses, traders may feel compelled to chase their losses by taking on more significant risks. This behavior often leads to a downward spiral, where emotional decisions replace strategic thinking, resulting in even greater losses.

3. Compromised Trading Plans: When traders risk too much, they may abandon their trading plans and strategies in a desperate attempt to recover. This abandonment often leads to poor decision-making and further financial setbacks.

Real-Life Example: A Cautionary Tale
Let me share a cautionary tale that illustrates the importance of only risking what you can afford to lose:
In my early trading days, I encountered a promising investment opportunity that seemed too good to pass up. I was convinced that I could achieve substantial profits quickly. Ignoring my established risk management principles, I decided to invest a significant portion of my savings—money that was meant for living expenses and future investments.
At first, everything appeared to be going smoothly as the investment initially performed well. However, unforeseen market events caused the value of my investment to plummet. I found myself in a precarious position, feeling the weight of my financial exposure. Panic set in as I realized that I had overextended myself, risking funds I could not afford to lose.
Desperate to recover my losses, I made impulsive decisions, leading to even more significant losses. It took me months to regain my financial footing, and I learned a hard lesson about the importance of responsible risk management.
From that experience, I committed to only risking what I could afford to lose. I recalibrated my trading strategies, created

a dedicated trading budget, and strictly adhered to my risk management rules. This commitment has since served me well, allowing me to navigate the markets with confidence and resilience.

Conclusion: Embracing Responsible Risk Management
In conclusion, the principle of risking only what you can afford to lose is a fundamental aspect of successful trading. This habit not only protects your capital but also enhances your decision-making capabilities and emotional well-being.

By adopting this approach, you create a safety net that allows you to trade with confidence, focus on your strategies, and weather the inevitable ups and downs of the market. Remember that trading is a journey, and maintaining responsible risk management practices is key to achieving your financial goals.

As you continue your trading journey, prioritize this principle and embrace the mindset of only risking what you can afford to lose. This commitment will serve you well in the long run, allowing you to thrive in the ever-changing world of trading.

HABIT 9: REVIEW AND REFLECT ON EVERY TRADE

"To grow as a trader, always review and reflect on each trade; every experience holds a lesson that can shape your future success."-GODFX

In the dynamic world of trading, the journey to success is not solely defined by profits and losses; it's shaped by continuous improvement and learning from past experiences. One of the most powerful habits that can set you on the path to becoming a highly effective trader is the practice of reviewing and reflecting on every trade. This chapter delves into the significance of post-trade analysis and how it can transform your trading approach.

The Importance of Post-Trade Analysis

Post-trade analysis involves reviewing each trade you execute, regardless of whether it results in a profit or a loss. Here are several reasons why this practice is crucial:

1. Learning Opportunities: Each trade presents a unique opportunity to learn. Analyzing what went well or what went wrong provides insights that can inform future decisions and strategies.

2. Identifying Patterns: By consistently reviewing your trades, you can identify patterns in your behavior and performance. This awareness allows you to recognize strengths and weaknesses in your trading style, leading to targeted improvements.

3. Enhancing Discipline: Regularly reviewing your trades reinforces discipline and encourages you to stick to your trading plan. It holds you accountable for your decisions and helps ensure that you remain committed to your strategy.

4. Emotion Regulation: Reflecting on your trades helps you detach from the emotional highs and lows associated with trading. By analyzing trades objectively, you can develop a more rational mindset that minimizes the impact of emotions on your trading decisions.
Methods for Effective Trade Review

To maximize the benefits of post-trade analysis, consider the following methods:

1. Maintain a Trading Journal: Keeping a detailed trading journal is one of the most effective ways to document your trades and analyze your performance. Record key details, including the trade setup, entry and exit points, reasons for entering the trade, and the outcome. Reflect on what you could have done differently and what you learned from the experience.

2. Evaluate Trade Performance: After each trade, assess your performance based on specific metrics. Analyze your win-loss ratio, risk-reward ratio, and the average time held in trades. This quantitative analysis can help you identify areas for improvement and refine your strategies.

3. Use Visual Aids: Incorporating charts and visual aids can enhance your analysis. Annotate charts with notes about your thought process at the time of the trade, identifying key technical indicators, market conditions, and emotional states. This visual representation can help you better understand your decision-making.

4. Seek Feedback and Mentorship: Consider sharing your trade reviews with a mentor or trading community. Gaining external perspectives can provide valuable insights and highlight blind spots you may not have considered.

5. Regularly Schedule Review Sessions: Dedicate time each week or month for comprehensive review sessions. During these sessions, reflect on your overall performance, analyze patterns, and set actionable goals for improvement.

Psychological Aspects of Reviewing Trades

The practice of reviewing trades is not solely analytical; it also involves psychological factors that can significantly impact your trading mindset:

1. Emotional Resilience: The ability to objectively assess your trades fosters emotional resilience. By focusing on the learning aspect rather than solely on profits or losses, you cultivate a growth mindset that embraces challenges as opportunities for improvement.

2. Overcoming Cognitive Biases: Traders are often susceptible to cognitive biases that can cloud judgment. Regularly reviewing trades helps identify these biases—such as overconfidence or loss aversion—allowing you to develop strategies to counteract them.

3. Building Confidence: A thorough review process can enhance your confidence as a trader. By recognizing your strengths and understanding your areas for improvement, you can build a more positive self-image and trust in your decision-making abilities.

Real-Life Example: The Transformative Power of Reflection

Let me share a personal example that highlights the impact of reviewing and reflecting on trades:

Early in my trading journey, I encountered a series of losses that left me feeling frustrated and disheartened. Instead of analyzing my trades, I focused solely on recouping my losses, which only led to more impulsive and emotional trading decisions.

After a particularly challenging week, I decided to take a step back and review my trades. I meticulously documented each trade in my journal, reflecting on my decision-making process and the emotions I experienced. What I discovered was enlightening.

I noticed a pattern in my losses: I had a tendency to deviate from my trading plan during moments of frustration. I was chasing losses and making trades based on emotions rather than analysis. This revelation was a turning point for me.

Armed with this newfound awareness, I implemented stricter adherence to my trading plan and began conducting regular review sessions. Over time, my trading performance improved significantly, and I developed a more disciplined approach. This experience reinforced the importance of reflecting on every trade, transforming my mindset and boosting my overall success as a trader.

Conclusion: The Path to Continuous Improvement

In conclusion, reviewing and reflecting on every trade is a vital habit that can significantly enhance your trading performance. This practice allows you to learn from experiences, identify patterns, and make informed decisions that lead to continuous improvement.

By maintaining a trading journal, evaluating performance metrics, seeking feedback, and scheduling regular review sessions, you can create a structured approach to analyzing your trades. Additionally, acknowledging the psychological aspects of reflection fosters emotional resilience, builds confidence, and helps overcome cognitive biases.

Embrace the habit of reviewing and reflecting on your trades as an essential part of your trading journey. This commitment to continuous improvement will empower you to refine your strategies, adapt to changing market conditions, and ultimately achieve greater success as a trader.

HABIT 10: ADAPT AND INNOVATE

"In trading, adaptability is key; innovate continuously to stay ahead of the curve and seize new opportunities."-GODFX

In the fast-paced and ever-changing world of trading, one of the most crucial habits for sustained success is the ability to adapt and innovate. Markets are influenced by a multitude of factors—economic data, geopolitical events, technological advancements, and shifts in market sentiment—making it imperative for traders to stay flexible and open to change. This chapter delves into the significance of adaptability in trading and offers practical strategies for cultivating this essential habit.

The Importance of Adaptation in Trading

1. Market Evolution: Financial markets are not static; they evolve over time. What worked well in one market environment may not be effective in another. For example, trading strategies that performed admirably during a bullish market may fail during a bearish trend. Recognizing these shifts and adapting accordingly is essential for long-term success.

2. Technological Advancement: The rise of technology has transformed trading, introducing new tools, platforms, and data analytics. Traders who embrace these advancements and incorporate them into their strategies can gain a competitive edge. Ignoring technological changes can leave traders at a disadvantage.

3. Response to Unexpected Events: Unforeseen events, such as economic crises or geopolitical conflicts, can disrupt markets in unpredictable ways. Traders must be prepared to adjust their strategies in response to these events to minimize losses and seize new opportunities.

4. Personal Growth and Learning: Adaptation is also about personal growth as a trader. By being open to new ideas and methodologies, you expand your knowledge base, refine your skills, and enhance your overall trading performance.

Cultivating the Habit of Adaptation and Innovation

To effectively adapt and innovate in your trading approach, consider the following strategies:

1. Embrace Continuous Learning: Make it a habit to stay informed about market trends, economic developments, and emerging trading technologies. Attend webinars, read books, and engage with trading communities. The more knowledge you acquire, the better equipped you'll be to adapt to changing market conditions.

2. Regularly Review and Update Strategies: Take time to assess your trading strategies periodically. Analyze their performance and determine whether they are still relevant in the current market environment. If not, don't hesitate to modify or replace them with new approaches that align with evolving conditions.

3. Experiment with New Techniques: Don't be afraid to explore and test new trading techniques and methodologies. Paper trading is an excellent way to experiment without risking real capital. This experimentation allows you to identify what works best for you and your trading style.

4. Stay Agile: In trading, being agile means being able to pivot quickly when the market changes. Develop a mindset that embraces change rather than resisting it. This agility can involve modifying your trading plan, adjusting position sizes, or exploring different asset classes.

5. Utilize Technology: Leverage technology to enhance your trading strategies. Use advanced charting software, algorithmic trading systems, or market analysis tools to gain insights and improve your decision-making processes. Staying updated with trading technology can give you an advantage in the market.

6. Network with Other Traders: Engaging with fellow traders can provide fresh perspectives and innovative ideas. Join trading forums, attend seminars, or participate in trading competitions. Collaboration and discussion can spark creativity and lead to new approaches you might not have considered.

Real-Life Example: Adapting to Market Changes
To illustrate the power of adaptation in trading, let's consider a real-life example:
During the COVID-19 pandemic, financial markets experienced unprecedented volatility. Many traditional trading strategies were rendered ineffective as investor sentiment shifted dramatically. One trader I know, who relied primarily on fundamental analysis, faced significant losses as the market dynamics changed overnight.
Recognizing the need for change, this trader decided to embrace technical analysis and incorporate various indicators to adapt to the rapidly evolving market conditions. He spent hours studying price action, identifying key support and resistance levels, and employing new strategies, such as short selling and options trading.
As he adapted to the changing landscape, he also innovated by

integrating risk management techniques into his trading plan, including tighter stop-loss orders and more precise position sizing. This flexibility and willingness to learn from the shifting environment allowed him to not only recover his losses but also achieve consistent profits as the market stabilized.

The Psychological Aspect of Adaptation
Adapting and innovating in trading also involves psychological factors that can significantly impact your mindset and decision-making:

1. Overcoming Fear of Change: Many traders fear change due to the uncertainty it brings. Embracing adaptability requires overcoming this fear and recognizing that change is an inherent part of trading. By adopting a growth mindset, you can view change as an opportunity for improvement rather than a threat.

2. Fostering Resilience: Adaptation is closely tied to resilience. When faced with losses or challenging market conditions, resilient traders are better equipped to bounce back and adjust their strategies. Cultivating resilience helps you maintain focus and confidence during turbulent times.

3. Embracing a Growth Mindset: Adapting and innovating requires a growth mindset—a belief that abilities and intelligence can be developed through dedication and hard work. By cultivating this mindset, you can approach challenges with curiosity and creativity, leading to continuous improvement in your trading.

Conclusion: The Path to Success through Adaptation
In conclusion, the habit of adapting and innovating is vital for achieving long-term success in trading. As markets evolve, traders must be willing to reassess their strategies, embrace new methodologies, and remain open to change.
By cultivating adaptability, leveraging technology, and

maintaining a commitment to continuous learning, you can position yourself for success in an ever-changing market environment. Remember, the key to thriving as a trader lies not in clinging to outdated methods but in embracing the journey of growth, learning, and innovation.

As you continue your trading journey, prioritize the habit of adaptation and innovation. This commitment will empower you to navigate the complexities of the market, seize opportunities, and ultimately achieve your financial goals.

EPILOGUE

As we conclude this exploration of the 10 habits of highly effective traders, I hope you've gained valuable insights that resonate with your own trading journey. These habits are not mere checklists; they are foundational principles that, when integrated into your daily routine, can lead to transformative results.

Throughout this book, we've discussed the importance of discipline, risk management, continuous learning, and maintaining a resilient mindset. Each of these habits plays a vital role in shaping your success as a trader, and I encourage you to reflect on how you can apply them in your practice.

Trading is a dynamic and often unpredictable endeavor, but it is also one of the most rewarding journeys one can undertake. With the right habits, you can navigate the challenges of the market with confidence and clarity. Remember, the path to becoming a highly effective trader is not a sprint but a marathon; it requires patience, persistence, and a commitment to lifelong learning.

As you move forward, I challenge you to embrace a mindset of growth. Celebrate your successes, learn from your mistakes, and continuously refine your approach. Surround yourself with a supportive community of fellow traders who share your passion, and seek out opportunities to expand your knowledge.

Ultimately, trading is not just about the profits you make but the person you become in the process. The habits you cultivate will shape not only your trading results but also your overall perspective on challenges and opportunities in life.

Thank you for joining me on this journey. I wish you success and fulfillment in your trading endeavors. May the habits you adopt today pave the way for a prosperous tomorrow.

— GODFX

AFTERWORD

As we reach the end of this book, I want to take a moment to reflect on the journey we've shared and to express my heartfelt gratitude to each of you for being a part of it. Writing "10 Habits of Highly Effective Traders" has been an incredibly rewarding experience, allowing me to distill the lessons I've learned through years of trading and share them with you.

I want to emphasize that the habits we've discussed are not just theoretical concepts; they are practical strategies that have been tested in the real world. They are tools that you can apply to your trading practice, helping you to navigate the complexities of the financial markets with confidence and clarity. Embrace them, adapt them to your own style, and make them a part of your daily routine.

I would also like to extend my appreciation to those who have supported me along the way—mentors, fellow traders, and the vibrant trading community that inspires continuous growth and learning. Your insights and encouragement have shaped my journey, and I hope to pay that forward by empowering others to achieve their trading goals.

As you move forward in your trading endeavors, remember that the path to success is paved with perseverance, discipline, and a willingness to learn. Each trade is an opportunity for growth, and every setback is a chance to refine your approach. Embrace this journey with an open mind and a resilient spirit.

I encourage you to stay curious, seek knowledge, and connect with other traders. The world of trading is ever-evolving, and being part of a supportive community can make all the difference. Share your experiences, learn from others, and continue to develop the habits that will lead you to long-term success.

Thank you for allowing me to share my insights with you. I look forward to hearing about your own journeys and the successes that await you as you implement these habits in your trading practice. May your future be filled with opportunities and achievements.

Wishing you all the best in your trading journey!

— GODFX

ACKNOWLEDGEMENT

As I reflect on the journey of writing this book, I am filled with gratitude for the many individuals who have supported and inspired me along the way.

First and foremost, I want to thank my family for their unwavering encouragement and belief in my vision. Your support has been a constant source of motivation, reminding me that pursuing my passion for trading and education is worthwhile.

I would like to extend my heartfelt appreciation to my mentors and peers in the trading community. Your insights, advice, and camaraderie have enriched my understanding of the markets and reinforced the importance of discipline and continuous learning. A special thank you to GODFX, whose guidance helped shape my approach and instilled in me the habits that are essential for success.

To the traders I've had the privilege of working with and learning from over the years—thank you for sharing your experiences and challenges. Each of you has contributed to my growth as a trader and as an educator, and I hope to pass on what I've learned to the next generation of traders.

I also want to acknowledge the countless authors, educators, and thought leaders whose work has influenced my thinking. Your dedication to sharing knowledge has inspired me to do the same and to contribute to the conversation about effective trading practices.

Lastly, I want to thank you, the reader. Your commitment to improving your trading skills and seeking out knowledge is commendable. I hope this book serves as a valuable resource on your journey toward becoming a highly effective trader.

Thank you all for being part of this endeavor. Your support has made this book possible, and I am excited to see how these habits will impact your trading journey.

— GODFX

ABOUT THE AUTHOR

Godfx

GODFX is a highly successful trader and financial educator with over a decade of experience in the financial markets. With a background that spans various trading styles—including day trading, swing trading, and long-term investing—GODFX has developed a unique approach to navigating the complexities of the trading world.

Driven by a passion for helping others succeed, GODFX has dedicated much of their career to sharing valuable insights and lessons learned from both triumphs and setbacks. Through a combination of analytical rigor and psychological resilience, they have cultivated a reputation for understanding not just the mechanics of trading but also the mindset required for success.

Having faced the challenges and pitfalls that many traders encounter, GODFX understands the importance of mastering effective habits. Their commitment to continuous learning and personal growth has led to a wealth of knowledge that they are eager to share with aspiring traders.

As a sought-after speaker and mentor, GODFX has inspired countless individuals to adopt disciplined trading practices and cultivate the habits necessary for long-term success in the markets. This ebook is the culmination of years of experience, research, and reflection, aimed at providing readers with practical strategies to enhance their trading effectiveness.

When not trading or educating others, GODFX enjoys engaging with the trading community, exploring new market trends, and continuously refining their own trading strategies. They believe that trading is not just a profession but a lifelong journey of learning and self-discovery.

PRAISE FOR AUTHOR

GODFX is a true visionary in the world of trading. His deep knowledge, passion, and commitment to sharing his expertise have not only transformed his own life but continue to inspire countless others on their trading journeys.
— ANONYMOUS

A masterful guide! GODFX breaks down complex trading concepts into simple, actionable steps. His insights into building a legacy through trading are both profound and practical. This book is a must-read for anyone serious about financial freedom.
— ANONYMOUS

GODFX's approach to trading is as empowering as it is effective. He not only teaches how to succeed in the markets but how to grow as a person. This is more than a book about trading; it's about building a life of purpose.
—ANONYMOUS

Rarely do you find someone as dedicated to helping others achieve their potential in trading as GODFX. His passion for teaching and sharing his knowledge is evident in every chapter. This book will change the way you view trading.
—ANONYMOUS

BOOKS IN THIS SERIES

The Trading Matrix: Breaking The Code To Financial Freedom

Imagine a world where the financial markets are no longer a mystery, but a matrix of opportunities waiting to be unlocked. In The Trading Matrix, GODFX pulls back the curtain on the complex systems that drive market movements, revealing a hidden code that, when understood, can unlock the path to financial freedom. This groundbreaking guide breaks away from traditional trading books, offering a fresh perspective on the art and science of profitable trading. Whether you're a beginner or an experienced trader, this book will challenge everything you think you know about the markets and provide you with the strategies, tools, and mindset needed to decode the market's secrets and achieve consistent success. Are you ready to break free and master The Trading Matrix?

10 Habits Of Highly Effective Traders

BOOKS BY THIS AUTHOR

10 Habits Of Highly Effective Traders

BOOKS BY THIS AUTHOR

10 Habits Of Highly Effective Traders

Unlock Your Trading Potential with "10 Habits of Highly Effective Traders"!

Are you ready to elevate your trading game? In this essential guide, GODFX, a seasoned trader with over a decade of experience, reveals the ten crucial habits that distinguish successful traders from the rest. Drawing from personal experiences and hard-won lessons, this book provides practical strategies that can transform your trading approach and lead to lasting success.

What You'll Learn:·

Discipline and Consistency: Discover how maintaining a disciplined mindset can enhance your decision-making and help you stick to your trading plan, even in volatile markets.

Risk Management: Learn essential techniques for managing risk effectively, ensuring that you protect your capital while maximizing your potential returns.

Continuous Learning: Embrace the importance of lifelong learning in trading, including how to stay informed about market trends and improve your skills.

Emotional Resilience: Develop the psychological strength needed to navigate the emotional ups and downs of trading, allowing you to make sound decisions under pressure.

Adaptability: Understand the necessity of being flexible and adapting your strategies to the ever-changing market environment.

Whether you are a novice trader looking to build a solid foundation or an experienced trader seeking to refine your approach, "10 Habits of Highly Effective Traders" provides actionable insights that will empower you to reach new heights in your trading journey.

Join thousands of successful traders who have transformed their trading practices with these essential habits. Take the first step toward mastering the art of trading today!

Get your copy now and unlock the habits that lead to trading success!

UNTITLED

The markets are more than a collection of numbers; they mirror our decisions, values, and aspirations. In trading, we pursue more than profit—we strive to create opportunities, inspire others, and build a lasting legacy for future generations of traders. Each trade represents a step toward shaping the future we envision.

www.ingramcontent.com/pod-product-compliance
Lightning Source LLC
Chambersburg PA
CBHW070346230526
45471CB00006B/2441